The Self-Hypnosis Formula

The Technique to Hypnotize Yourself into Hypnotic Realities, Meditation, Lucid Dreaming, Sleep and More

by Max Trance

DISCLAIMER

Nothing in this work is psychological advice, medical advice, financial advice or any other kind of advice. It is important to seek advice from an appropriately qualified medical professional whenever you have any kind of medical issue. And if you are undergoing psychological treatment, it may be best to discuss with your specialist before implementing any of the processes contained within this book.

The material in this work is for entertainment purposes only, and you may not be entertained.

Your use of the material in this work is entirely at your own risk. The author, publisher, and all other entities associated with the creation, sale, distribution and everything else to do with this work make no representations or warranties of any kind with regard to this work or its contents.

Table of Contents

Introduction

I was skeptical. I was in the middle of reading a book on scientific experiments that no-one yet knew how to explain. And where it was cheap enough to do so, I was running the experiments, just to see what happened.

I was getting some unexpected results. In short, everything in the book worked just like the author said it would.

As a budding scientist, this was fascinating to me.

Then I came across the most outrageous experiment of all. Do this one thing, it claimed, and you will be able to experience visual hallucinations.

Ridiculous! I thought.

But I ran the experiment anyway.

You can imagine my astonishment when less than 2 hours later, I was experiencing full-blown visual hallucinations. In the beginning, it was just something tiny. With my eyes closed, I could clearly see an orange that wasn't there. But it was a start. And I was hooked.

The process that was outlined in that book was a simple self-hypnosis induction. Essentially it was advocating what hypnotists would view as a variant of the eye fixation induction.

While it worked for me, and got me started down the path to hypnosis, there are other pathways to self-hypnosis that I've found to be much more effective.

In this book, we'll cover what I've found to be the easiest and most reliable way to induce self-hypnosis on-demand. We'll also go over what kinds of things you can do with self-hypnosis, and how to do them. And finally, we'll cover how to make those changes stick and how to verify that it's worked.

My aim with this book is to get you started with self-hypnosis fast, so I've made it as short as I possibly can.

Why use self-hypnosis

So there I was. I could feel my heart pounding in my chest. My breathing was all over the place, quick and shallow. And my thoughts were a total mess. Running around in loops.

I was in the grips of a panic attack. Totally freaking out.

And then I remembered something.

I am The Hypnotist.

Capital T. Capital H.

I took a slow, deep breath, and allowed my attention to move to the physical sensations within my body.

I noticed how my hands were clenched into claws, and became curious about what that was like.

I explored how the sensations changed as I noticed different parts of my body.

I became aware of the tension in my shoulders, and noticed that in that moment even my toes were tense.

As my attention wandered through the various physical sensations I was experiencing, I felt peace begin to spread over me.

And within less than 3 minutes, I had fully restored my usual calm.

All the tension was gone, my heart had stopped trying to escape from my chest, and I was feeling serene.

The process that I followed was a simple self-hypnosis technique.

Milton Erickson is generally regarded as one of the greatest hypnotists of all time. Throughout the course of his life he ran countless hypnotic experiments. He wanted to know exactly what kinds of problems could be helped with the use of hypnosis.

Ultimately his work resulted in what we know today as hypnotherapy.

In hypnotherapy, we use our knowledge of hypnosis to help people to overcome all kinds of problems.

The scope here is vast. In essence, any problem that is in some way caused by a pattern inside the mind can potentially be helped.

To give you some ideas, this includes things like:

- Overcoming social anxiety.
- Overcoming all kinds of fears and phobias such as:
    - Fear of heights.
    - Fear of dogs.
    - Fear of flying.
    - Fear of missing out.
- Stopping in-progress panic attacks.
- Changing compulsive behaviors.
- Building motivation.
- Building confidence.
- Achieving goals.
- Losing weight and keeping it off.
- Quitting smoking.
- Breaking other addictions.
- Pain control.
- And much, much more.

Beyond fixing problems, hypnosis itself can be used for fun.

When we're hypnotizing others for entertainment, generally we want them to act out something. This could be gluing them in place, having them talk like an alien, having them perform strange activities such as playing an air piano, or just about anything we can imagine that seems like it might be funny.

When we're hypnotizing ourselves for our amusement, the fun takes on a different quality. While we could hypnotize ourselves to act out any of those things for the entertainment of an audience, a big part of a hypnosis show is that the audience thinks the hypnotist is making them do it.

Naturally it's nowhere near as compelling to an external audience when we make ourselves do something.

So how can we use hypnosis in the context of our own entertainment? As with overcoming problems, the possibilities here are near endless.

Again, to give you some ideas, the entertainment possibilities include:

- The vacation of our dreams.
- A gateway into lucid dreaming.
- A gateway into meditation.
- Modifying our perception of video games to make them seem real.
- Making ourselves drunk on water.
- And much, much more.

Now it might seem like fixing problems of the mind, and massively extending our repertoire for fun might be reason enough.

But wait! There's more! As they say in the TV commercials.

Not only can we use self-hypnosis to overcome a vast array of problems, and for our own entertainment, we can also use it to hone our skills in just about any area we might choose.

With self-hypnosis we can increase our focus, and distort our perception of the flow of time, which makes for a learning environment in which we can quickly get massive results.

Need to study for an exam? Simply drop yourself into hypnosis, engage a bit of time distortion, and spend a few hours mentally revising the entire course in detail. All in the space of a few minutes of clock time.

Want to practice a piece of music? Once again, drop yourself into hypnosis, engage your time distortion, and methodically work through that piece over and over again until you've got it perfect.

Perhaps you'd like to run through a critical presentation? You'd never guess this, but all you do is drop yourself into hypnosis, engage your time distortion, spin up a hallucination, and do the presentation over and over again, until you've got it just right.

You're probably beginning to spot a pattern here.

So to recap, there are three huge areas where self-hypnosis can rapidly lead to huge gains:

1. Overcoming problems of the mind.
2. Enhancing the fun things we do.
3. Supercharging our ability to learn new things.

And of course, there's one final place where self-hypnosis excels: when you're a hypnotist and want to hypnotize others, it's always a good idea to go into hypnosis yourself first.

With all of that in mind, it's natural to ask a question.

What exactly is hypnosis?

What is hypnosis

The short answer is that no-one really knows.

What we do know is that hypnosis is a state in which the mind becomes more open to new experiences. Essentially, in hypnosis we partially or completely shut down the part of the mind that inhibits new stuff from going in.

And when we're unimpeded by all the things we already know, we can often learn much more quickly and effectively.

This is why hypnosis is useful for helping us to overcome problems, for supercharging our ability to learn new things, and for helping us to let go of reality for a bit so that we can have more fun.

For the purposes of this book, I'm going to use the following definition of hypnosis:

Hypnosis is what happens when our conscious attention is consumed to the extent that we cannot interfere with the changes we'd like to have happen.

How we do that to ourselves is what the rest of this book is about.

What is self-hypnosis

In regular hypnosis, the hypnotist guides their subject firstly into hypnosis, and then into the changes they'd like to have happen.

Since the hypnotist can be conscious and aware of what's going on while the subject's unconscious mind is tweaked, this might seem like a perfect combination.

And when we're working at the level where we have to think our way through how to solve specific problems, this is certainly the case.

Now it might seem that this would make it impossible achieve meaningful change with self-hypnosis. After all, if the hypnotist knows what's going on, won't they interfere with their own changes?

Luckily there are other, more elegant, ways.

In self-hypnosis, we are both the hypnotist and the subject.

For our purposes here, I'm going to define self-hypnosis like this:

Self-hypnosis is what happens when we work through a process that's designed to consume our conscious attention, resulting in us being fully absorbed in the experience.

Conveniently, there are many ways that we can do this. Our brains have physical limitations around how much they can process at once, and as a result our minds have limitations on how many things we can focus on at the same time.

And the beautiful thing is that when we use processes that are designed to exploit these limitations, we're highly likely to end up in a state of self-hypnosis.

Here's the truth:

When we follow the processes correctly, our brains simply don't have the resources to not go into hypnosis.

So how do we get started?

How to hypnotize yourself

As I mentioned earlier, there are many ways that we can hypnotize ourselves. In this book, I'm going to give just one way.

When you're hypnotizing others, you'll want to have your eyes open, so the process I give here can be done with your eyes open or closed.

To begin with though, do it with your eyes closed.

Now, this process has quite a few steps. You won't be able to remember them all at first. The human mind just doesn't have that capacity.

So what you'll need to do is break it down.

The overall structure looks like this:

1. Get yourself comfortable.
2. Do some stuff with your breathing to focus and calm your mind.
3. Start to deepen the process by moving your attention outwards.
4. Induce hypnosis by directing your attention to your left hand and fingers.
5. Deepen the hypnosis by moving your attention all the way out to the things around you, then down into one specific thing.
6. Find a pathway to your hypnotic reality by expanding your attention outwards again, and then allowing your pathway to form in front of you.
7. Travel down your pathway, find the gateway into your hypnotic reality, and step inside.

We'll work through each of these steps, one at a time. With each step, practice it a few times before moving onto the next one, so that you're starting to turn it into a habit.

Step 1 – Get yourself comfortable

In the very first step, we're setting up our environment so that things are optimal.

As with all hypnosis, get rid of any distractions. This might include turning off TV and radio, disabling notifications on your devices, putting any pets out of the room, asking others not to disturb you, and anything else that might be needed.

After you've created a quiet space to practice, work through this process a few times. As a rule, it's usually a good idea to carry out the steps at least three times in sequence. If you find yourself forgetting, work through it more times until you don't.

Also, it's important to be aware that it's possible to fall asleep when running through these processes, so if you have to be somewhere later on today, make sure you set an alarm.

Do this exercise now:

1. Find somewhere comfortable and safe to lie down.
2. If it's easy to do so, elevate your feet slightly above your head.
3. Close your eyes.

After closing your eyes, luxuriate in the peace and quiet for a few moments, before opening your eyes and either repeating the exercise, or continuing to read on.

Step 2 – Focus your mind

Next, it's time to move your attention inwards. We do this with a simple breathing exercise.

Each step in this self-hypnosis process will build on the previous steps, so the very first step will always be to do all of the previous steps.

Each time we run the process, we start with closing our eyes, and end with opening them.

1. Get yourself comfortable. Lie down and close your eyes.
2. Notice your breathing. Don't try to do anything with it, just notice it.
3. Focus your attention on one small part of your breathing. This can be anything you choose. It might be the feeling of your clothes moving ever so slightly against your skin as your chest rises and falls. It might be the way the tension in your shoulders shifts as you breathe in and breathe out. Or the sound that you make as you breathe. Whatever it is, focus your attention on just one small part of your breathing.
4. Follow that one small part of your breathing for three breaths. Don't try to do anything with it. Just be curious. And notice.
5. Bask in the glow of that calm for a few moments.

After following that one small part of your breathing, being curious, and noticing, bask in that for a few moments before opening your eyes.

As with getting yourself comfortable, it's important to repeat the entire process from beginning to end a few times. That means everything from closing your eyes through to opening your eyes at the end.

Repeat three times, then move on to the next step.

Step 3 – Start to deepen the process

For the next exercise, we want to begin to deepen the effects. We do this by moving our attention outwards to the many, many things in the universe that aren't us.

1. Get yourself comfortable, and focus your mind with the breathing exercise from the previous steps.
2. Allow your attention to move outside of your body into the objects around you. This can be walls, furniture, trees, the ground, or anything else. The key point here is that it is not just one, but many.
3. Bask in that for a few moments, noticing all of those things around you.
4. Bring your attention back to your body.

As with the other steps, repeat 3 times before moving on to the next step.

Step 4 – Induce hypnosis

Now it's time to induce the hypnosis itself. Depending on how good you are at experiencing hypnosis, you may already be there. Since I have no way of knowing this, and if you're beginning, nor do you, work through the formal hypnotic induction in this exercise to induce hypnosis.

As with the other steps, we begin with closing your eyes and working through the other steps in sequence, followed by the induction, before we open our eyes at the end.

1. Get yourself comfortable, do your breathing exercises, then move your attention outwards before bringing it back to your body.
2. Notice your left hand. Pay attention to all the sensations in that left hand. Temperatures. Pressures. Tensions. How that hand moves. Notice everything you can about the details.
3. Wriggle the fingers on that left hand and notice how they move. Do this for a few seconds. If they won't move at all, don't worry: that just means you've already gone into hypnosis.
4. Wriggle those fingers half as much, and half as much again. Move them as slowly as possible. Really focus all of your attention on moving those fingers by the least amount you can, as slowly as you can. Do this for a few moments until those fingers feel like they won't move.

How do you move your hand again?

It's actually really easy. After verifying that you cannot move your hand at all, you simply decide to move it. In the event it's stuck, just shake your head to clear the hypnosis and you'll find that you can move easily.

Hypnosis is a natural state, so to come out of it, all you have to do is open your eyes and move your attention to the things around you.

Step 5 – Deepen the hypnosis

By now you should be able to comfortably move yourself into hypnosis more or less on-demand by following the previous exercises.

If you can't do that yet, it's just a matter of practice.

Like every other skill that you've ever learnt, it will be slow and clunky at first, but you'll quickly learn and become good at it.

Once you can induce hypnosis in yourself on-demand, the next step is to deepen that hypnosis.

This is the part where we begin to effectively knock your conscious mind out of the way enough that you can achieve whatever it is that you want to achieve, so it's critical for your success.

As with the other steps, run through the previous processes first, add in the new steps, then open your eyes and bring yourself out of hypnosis at the end.

1. Get yourself comfortable, do your breathing exercises, move your attention outwards, bring your attention back to your body, then focus on your left hand and wriggle those fingers slower and slower to induce hypnosis.
2. Move your attention outwards again, to all the things around you.
3. Out of all those things around you, choose just one thing, and go inside it. Take a few moments to experience the world as that thing. I find that trees are very handy here, so if you're a tree, feel your roots reaching down into the ground, and the sun on your leaves.

4. Bask in the experience of being that thing for a few moments. Be curious and allow fascination to flow through you.

To come out of this one, move your attention back into your body, notice all of the sensations, breathe in deeply, and open your eyes, wide awake and alert.

As with the other steps, practice a few times to make sure you've got it.

Step 6 – Find a pathway

Next up, we're going to blatantly steal something from shamanism. We've induced hypnosis and deepened it, so it's time to do something with it.

This is where we start to move onto actually doing something with the hypnosis. Don't worry just yet about what shape that might take on. We'll get to that in a later chapter. For now, we just want to get the process down so that you can use it.

Once again, run through the previous processes, add in the new steps, then open your eyes and bring yourself out of hypnosis at the end.

1. Get yourself comfortable, do your breathing exercises, move your attention outwards, bring your attention back to your body, and induce hypnosis by slowing your fingers right down. Next, find everything around you, become just one of those things, and be that thing for a little while.
2. Allow your attention to move outwards again, this time going out further than ever before. Discover how far out your attention can go. Become aware of everything around you.
3. As you're exploring all of that, allow a pathway to form in front of you. This could take on any form at all. It might be a path through a forest, or a corridor, a tunnel, or anything else. You'll know it when you find it.
4. When the pathway has taken shape, step inside.
5. Look around that pathway and notice all the details. The colors. The textures. Is there an aroma? What qualities does your pathway have?

As you go deeper into hypnosis, you may find that it becomes progressively more difficult to come out of it again. This is a good sign.

Know that at any time you can always come out of hypnosis by doing nothing more than shifting your focus back into yourself and orienting yourself to your physical location.

If you find yourself needing a break, remember that you can take breaks at any time. That's part of the reason I've broken this process down into 7 easy steps.

Step 7 – Step inside your hypnotic reality

We're almost there now.

You've learnt to still your mind, to move your attention about, to induce hypnosis, to deepen your hypnosis, and finally to step onto a pathway.

Naturally the next step is to walk down that pathway. Now when I say walk, you can use any means of traveling that you prefer. Maybe you'll fly. Perhaps you'll swim. You might even teleport, or drive a motorcycle.

What usually happens for me is that some means of transportation appears in front of me, so I use that.

In this step, you'll be stepping inside a hypnotic reality. Don't worry about what that might be just yet. That's for a later chapter. For now, it's enough to step inside it and notice what's there.

Even if it's just a void for now.

Or an entire world.

So to begin, run through all the previous 6 steps

1. Get yourself comfortable, do your breathing exercises, move your attention outwards, bring your attention back to your body, and induce hypnosis by slowing your fingers right down. Next, find everything around you, become just one of those things, and be that thing for a little while. Move your attention outwards again, and look around until you find your pathway. Then inspect the details of your pathway. Get a sense of what your pathway's like.
2. Travel down your pathway by whatever means seems right to you, until you come to a door or gateway of some kind.

3. Examine the door or gateway, then step through that.
4. Allow your hypnotic reality to form around you.

When you arrive inside your hypnotic reality, you can allow yourself to spend as long there as you like.

And when you're ready to come back out of hypnosis, look around and find your pathway, travel back down it the way you came, orient yourself back into your body, open your eyes, and look around your physical location.

From now on throughout this book, whenever we're talking about things you can do I will refer to this entire process by saying something like *hypnotize yourself and step inside your hypnotic reality.*

Don't panic!

Searing pain screamed up my spine and down my legs. I was paralyzed with agony to the extent that for a few seconds, I couldn't even move.

Even when the pain settled down, it was still so intense that I couldn't stand.

I dragged myself along the floor to my bedroom and lay down on my bed. No matter how I moved or oriented myself, I just couldn't make that pain go away.

The pain passed eventually, but it kept on coming back every 4 or 5 years, getting worse each time.

That first time I experienced sciatic back pain, it was gone the very next day.

The next time, a few years later, things had clearly deteriorated, because it lasted a few days.

Each time I had an attack, the pain would get worse. And it would persist for longer. The first attack lasted for a single evening. The last one... almost a month.

My doctor had a cunning plan. *Just take these powerful painkillers for the rest of your life*, she said.

That didn't appeal to me very much, and even though I'd been a self-hypnotist for 20 years at that point, I'd never thought to look into pain control.

So I did some research, and as a result of that research built a simple hypnotic pain control process. Then I used a self-hypnosis process like the one you've just learnt to implement it within myself.

That was over 10 years ago, and I haven't had a single attack of sciatic back pain since. And as a side benefit, these days I never use pain-killers for anything.

Now I'm not going to cover how to do pain control here, because that's not what this book is about. I'll probably write about it at a later date, so if that's something you're interested in, please let me know.

When people tell me that they want specific stuff, it moves up my prioritization list.

The reason I tell you this story is to impress upon you just how effective self-hypnosis can be.

I went from being quite literally crippled by the pain, to having the occasional twinge every few years, with a simple self-hypnosis process.

We've already covered how to induce and deepen self-hypnosis, and how to move yourself into a state where you can make things happen.

In the rest of this book, we're going to cover how to do useful things with it.

The purpose of self-hypnosis

At the start of this book, I gave a short list of just a few of the areas where hypnosis can help.

If you recall, the broad areas were:

1. Overcoming problems of the mind.
2. Enhancing the fun things we do.
3. Supercharging our ability to learn new things.

As it turns out, most of these things are easily performed inside a hypnotic reality. That's why we created one in step 7 of our self-hypnosis process.

If you're wondering, a hypnotic reality is simply an environment in which you find yourself when you're in deep hypnosis. It can be anything from a total void, to an entire universe filled with detail.

And just like real reality, you can explore, learn, and do stuff there.

Earlier I mentioned time distortion. It's possible that as you were working through the steps to learn self-hypnosis, you noticed that it felt like a lot of time had passed, and then were surprised when you looked at a clock and noticed that it had been only a few minutes.

That's because the process you've learnt has significant amounts of time distortion built into it.

The rule is that the more details you notice on all scales, the more time you will perceive. Conveniently, observing as many details as possible also drives you further into hypnosis.

I'm not going to go into detail on everything you can do in hypnosis, because if I did, this book would be thousands of pages long. Or more.

Instead, we're going to cover a handful of processes that I've found to be universally useful.

We'll cover a universal pattern for causing change, how to use self-hypnosis to leap-frog into lucid dreaming, and how to use the in-built time distortion coupled with deliberate practice to hone our skills.

Hypnotic symbols

Before we move onto how to cause change, it's important to have a tiny amount of understanding on exactly how the mind works.

If you'd like to know more about this, I've covered the underlying processes in a lot more detail in my book **Artful Hypnotic Anchoring**.

For our purposes here, all we need to know is that unconscious change doesn't happen in a way that we'd normally perceive as being logical.

Instead, the way that changes happen is that we have two or more states, and they mix together.

In this context, states can be anything that can exist inside a mind. They could be memories, emotions, thoughts, or even our ongoing stream of experience.

Usually a state is comprised of all of the above.

For example, happiness is an emotion, but it's also coupled to all of our happy memories. When we're happy, we tend to think more thoughts about happy things. Because they're part of the state, our happy memories become more accessible than our other memories. And our ongoing stream of experience is generally happy.

The same is true of other states like anger, sadness, joy, and so on.

How do you get rid of sadness?

Most people when faced with that problem will try to logic their way out of it. This doesn't work, and will usually make the problem worse.

Instead, what we have to do to get rid of sadness is fire up some happy memories. Since these happy memories are more difficult to access when we're sad, it's often useful to use an anchor to do this.

An anchor is nothing more than something that reminds us of a certain state.

The really nice thing about all of this is that even though we don't necessarily know how any of this works, our brains implicitly do know. And because our brains implicitly know how this stuff works, a lot of the time, all we have to do to fix problems is get out of the way.

At the core of our minds, we solve problems by mixing the problem and solution together, until the problem has gone away. And because of how the system works, we don't even have to know what the solution might be.

When we're inside a hypnotic reality, these problems and their solutions are represented by unconscious symbols inside the reality. The symbols can be anything at all. They might appear to be related to the problem, or they might appear to be totally unrelated.

Examples of symbols that might appear include objects, people, creatures, concepts, actual symbols, and in general terms, anything else that can be described with a noun. If it has a name, it can be a symbol. And just like nouns, symbols can be modified by adjectives.

To illustrate this point, close your eyes for a moment, and imagine a fast car. Then imagine a slow car. Notice how they feel different. Even if it's the same car. So a fast car and a slow car could potentially be different symbols inside your mind.

Remember, at this level our brains don't work on logic. It's enough that there is some loose association between the symbol and whatever we'd like to change, even if we don't know what that association is.

The fact that the association exists is enough for our brains to sort things out for us.

How to plan change

The association process inside our minds has an important consequence for self-hypnosis: If we want to work on any problem in self-hypnosis, all we have to do is decide beforehand what problem we'd like to work on, and how we'd rather be.

We do this before we take ourselves into hypnosis.

The act of making this decision creates a framework for the unconscious symbols that our brain will inject into our hypnotic reality.

We still have to manipulate these symbols inside our hypnotic reality, but here's the thing: we're going to be manipulating stuff there anyway.

I know it probably seems absurdly simple, and I could write about this for a very long time if I wanted to, but that really is all there is to it.

The truth is, for our purposes here we don't really need anything more than that.

How to use self-hypnosis to get results fast

Now we have all the pieces in place, it's time for the overall process for doing useful work with self-hypnosis.

Here's what the basic process looks like:

1. Decide what you'd like the outcome from your self-hypnosis session to be.
2. Hypnotize yourself and step inside your hypnotic reality.
3. Look around for some symbols and allow them to move about so that they seem right.
4. Practice whatever you're here for at least three times. If you want, you can notice how your symbols shift and move while you're practicing. They're going to do that anyway, but sometimes it's interesting to watch.
5. Either bring yourself out of hypnosis, or drift off to sleep.

If you're wondering, the drifting off to sleep part is especially easy. All you have to do to fall asleep at that point is keep on exploring your hypnotic reality.

That's probably not quite clear yet, so let's go over a couple of worked examples.

Example 1 – Social anxiety

A huge problem that a lot of people experience is social anxiety.

Despite what it might seem like when we experience it, social anxiety is remarkably simple to fix.

At its core, social anxiety happens because we're not comfortable in social situations. The solution for this is to expose ourselves to enough such situations that we can begin to dissolve the anxiety.

But there's a problem.

If we try to do that in real life, we end up overwhelmed, and fire up the social anxiety patterns. This reinforces them and makes them worse.

We don't necessarily have any internal resources big enough to deal with the entire problem at once.

But we can certainly deal with a little bit of it.

The key is to move in tiny steps.

This is where self-hypnosis is brilliant. Because we're manipulating symbols inside a highly abstracted hypnotic reality, it feels totally safe to us. And at the same time, that safeness becomes attached to social situations out in real life.

Now I'm not going to claim that just one session is enough to fix any problem. There are far too many variables, even when you're working with a skilled hypnotherapist. This why many hypnotherapists won't book someone in for anything other than the simplest problems unless they're willing to sign up for 8 or more sessions.

In short: we want our customers to have a good experience.

Each time we do some work on the problem, it decreases a little.

Now as hypnotherapists, we never know how much work might be required to fix a specific problem. But we can make educated guesses.

Let me give you an example.

We know from experience that most smokers will quit after the first session. We also know that some won't, so we have them sign up for a 3 session program.

In doing this we achieve some important things. First, we get feedback and we can tell which customers have quit. Second, those who do quit after the first session feel like they've been really well looked after. And third, if someone still hasn't quit after 3 sessions, we can book them right back in for another, on the house, until we've fixed the problem.

Since almost all smokers have quit by the third session, we can massively increase the confidence in our service without it costing us much at all.

By the way, shameless plug time! If you're a smoker, and don't want to be, my book **The Quit Smoking Formula** contains a process designed to guide smokers through quitting and onto becoming non-smokers for life. And the best part? You can use the processes in this book you're reading right now to supercharge it.

Now, let's go back to our example of social anxiety.

The reality is that even though the solution is straightforward, some problems require more than one session to fix.

So that's the first thing: be aware that whatever problem you're working on, you're probably not going to get there in one session.

If a skilled hypnotherapist requires 8 sessions to work through something, you can reasonably expect that it will take you more than that when you do-it-yourself with self-hypnosis.

Naturally, some problems are smaller than others.

So how do we fix it?

First, we need to define the problem, and what we'd like to be different. Try to come up with specific situations where the problem happens. A specific situation is something like: *when I talk to the cashier at my local supermarket, I've felt anxious.*

The important characteristic here is that you can get a clear picture of an actual event in the real world, and what has been happening.

Next, we decide how we'd like it to be different: *when I talk to the cashier at my local supermarket, my shoulders will feel relaxed.*

Why just the shoulders? Well, you can make it as big or as small a change as you like. As a rule, smaller changes are easier to manifest than bigger ones.

And guess what happens when you stack up a dozen or more tiny changes?

That's right! The problem starts to become a thing of the past.

Once you've defined what's been happening, and what you'd like to have happen instead, it's time to run the process.

As before, run through the steps:

1. Hypnotize yourself, and follow the process to your hypnotic reality. As you're doing this, really bask in the effects along the way. Allow yourself to glow. When you're a tree, feel the

sun on your leaves and the energy of the nutrients flowing into you from the ground. The stronger you can make these positive feelings, the better. When you're glowing, follow the pathway and step inside your hypnotic reality.

2. Look around for some symbols and move them about so that they seem right. Don't concern yourself with what they might represent. Treat it more like a decorating exercise.

3. Since we're here to change our social anxiety, imagine stepping into the supermarket and talking to the cashier. Work through that process several times inside your mind, noticing how your shoulders relax more each time.

4. Either bring yourself out of hypnosis, or drift off to sleep.

And that's it. At that point, the session is done.

Of course, you still need to test, which is nothing more than placing yourself into the situation in real life, and noticing what happens.

So far as I can tell, this process is the core of all change, not just social anxiety. All effective techniques and solutions that I've used appear to have this structure on some level.

The key is to work on small things first, and work your way up.

Imagine for a moment if you were to buy a recipe book and try to make a gourmet meal. When most people do this, they don't get it even close to right the first time. But if they stick at it, before long they can effortlessly follow the recipe to success.

Working on problems inside your mind is just the same. Start off with small problems to practice, then move up to the bigger ones when you're confident in the process.

The easiest way to make this process fail is to jump straight onto a problem that's too big for now.

So don't do that.

Start with tiny things, and then slowly move up as you become more skilled. When you do this, you will get there in no time.

Example 2 – Learning to play piano

Next up, let's consider a honing a skill. In this case, we'll use the piano as an example, and the process applies equally to any other skill.

When we want to work with a skill, we need something for our brain to latch onto before we start. If we've never even tried to play a piano before, it's unlikely to work unless we're a very skilled hypnotist.

The same is true with study or any other kind of learning. If we want to study inside our hypnotic reality, we first must go over the material in real life. Similarly, if we want to improve a skill, it's important that we've had a little experience with using that skill.

Luckily this is easy to work around. The key word here is hone. We're not trying to create a new skill from scratch, just get better at one we already possess.

In the case of playing a piano, we've at least tried to belt out a few songs before, and we've attempted to read music and translate it into pressing the right keys in the right sequence with the right timing.

The basic information is already in our mind, we're just not using it optimally yet.

When you think about it, honing a skill is nothing more than another form of change. Change and learning are really just different words for the same thing.

So it follows that we can use the same process.

And it gets better. Remember that time distortion we built into the self-hypnosis process? When you want to hone a skill, you can decide to spend as much time as you'd like doing so.

As before, first we define the change that we'd like to have happen: *I'm going to spend 4 hours learning to play Let It Go on the piano, paying particular attention to properly synchronizing my foot movements with the piano keys. I will practice deliberately and methodically.*

By the way, self-hypnosis sessions can be supercharged even more by using deliberate practice.

Deliberate practice here is a specific type of practice in which rather than just repeating something over and over again, we pay attention to what we're doing. When make a mistake, we stop, go back a little, and redo the part where we made the mistake, slowly and methodically.

To make it concrete, suppose we're playing the piano and we hit the wrong note. With deliberate practice, we stop, go back a couple of bars, and slowly and methodically play through the next few bars.

Then we go back again, and speed up a little.

We repeat the process until we find ourselves automatically playing the correct note at the right speed and timing.

Then we go back one last time and continue playing through the rest of the piece. Or at least, until we make the next mistake.

By following this process, we can massively cut down our learning time since we're focusing only on the parts that need the most work.

So if you know how to do that, definitely use deliberate practice inside your hypnotic reality.

As with the social anxiety example, now we run through the steps:

1. Hypnotize yourself and step inside your hypnotic reality.
2. Look around for some symbols and move them about so that they seem right. Don't concern yourself with what they might represent. Treat it more like a decorating exercise.
3. Since we're here to practice playing the piano, look around for your piano. It will be there. You may have to look a little to find it. Then sit down and play for four hours. Just like you planned.
4. Either bring yourself out of hypnosis, or drift off to sleep.

And that's it. As with the previous example, at this point, the session is done.

In the case of honing skills, the test is that we then do the thing in real life and notice how much better we've become at whatever it might be.

Example 3 – Create a place to meditate

If you want to meditate inside your hypnotic reality, it can be a good idea to have a place to do it. To save effort, it's helpful to create this once, go back there a few times to reinforce it, and then use it at will in the future.

To create a place for meditation, write out a brief plan before you begin so that you have a clear picture of where you're going. This can be anything that you choose, so long as it is suitable for the kind of meditation you're planning to explore.

A typical plan might look something like:

When I enter my hypnotic reality, I will find myself drawn to a pathway through a forest and up a mountain. This pathway runs alongside a river. At the end of the pathway, 17 steps are hewn into the rock, leading to an ancient stone monastery. At the top of the steps are two giant doors. I open them, and step inside a hall with a vaulted ceiling. There are all kinds of rooms in the monastery that I can explore at any time, including a library and a courtyard with a fountain for contemplation.

It's important to not go into too much detail here. It's usually best to write just enough that the images start to form inside your mind. The key is that there should be something for your mind to latch onto, but lots of flexibility for your unconscious mind to create new things.

As the final sentence of your description, give your location a name. This can be anything at all, so long as it's easy for you to remember. You do this by writing a final sentence something like this:

From now on, my monastery will be known as K'ten.

Once you've created your meditation location, and given it a name, you can go back there any time you choose by simply referring to it by name.

The act of naming it attaches an anchor, just like the hypnotic symbols you've been using for change.

It is possible to do all of this once you've entered your hypnotic reality. And most people find that it's much easier when they write things out beforehand.

Beyond that, meditation works a lot like honing a skill.

After lying down (or sitting if you prefer), read your description and imagine your place of meditation. Get a sense of any details around how you're going to get there, and what it's like when you're there.

Not too much though. Just enough that you know you've got it inside your mind.

Then, look around your place of meditation in your imagination, and allow its name to form inside your mind.

K'ten.

Smile and nod. Take a slow, deep breath. And allow its name to resonate inside your mind.

K'ten.

The rule tends to be that whenever you want something to stick, it's a good idea to repeat it three times.

Now that you've got a plan for your place of meditation, it's time to get started with the hypnosis.

As with the other examples, work through the process to deepen the hypnosis, distort time, travel down your pathway into your hypnotic reality, and finally travel into your meditation location.

Here's the process:

1. Make yourself comfortable wherever you're planning to do the self-hypnosis.
2. Have a quick look at the description of your place of meditation, imagine it, and allow its name to resonate throughout your mind.
3. Smile and nod, then take a slow, deep breath.
4. Hypnotize yourself and step inside your hypnotic reality.
5. Look around for the pathway, and follow it to your place of meditation.
6. Standing at the entrance, allow the name of the place to saturate your mind as it resonates within you. *K'ten.*
7. Go inside, look around and explore for a bit.
8. When you've explored enough, wander out and back down the pathway to where you entered your hypnotic reality.
9. Bring yourself out of hypnosis.

Since you've created a specific location this time around, it's important to go back there a few times for no reason other than exploration. By this I mean run the entire process at least three times, from making yourself comfortable through to bringing yourself out of hypnosis.

Do this before you use it for meditation.

You will know when you've done it enough, because you'll find that you can get there quickly and easily almost as soon as you enter your hypnotic reality.

Also, it's important that you know your place of meditation well enough that you can get there using only its name, without looking at the description before you hypnotize yourself.

This tends to happen automatically after running through the process a few times.

Example 4 – Meditation

Depending on the kind of meditation you're planning, you may want to decide on a theme for your meditation before you begin. So if there's something specific that you'd like to achieve take a few moments to plan it out first.

If you've created somewhere to meditate, you can go there. Otherwise, just look around your hypnotic reality for a suitable spot.

It's probably becoming obvious by now, but here's the process:

1. Make yourself comfortable wherever you're planning to do the self-hypnosis.
2. If there's some specific purpose for your meditation, check your plan, and briefly call it up in your imagination to make sure that you're clear on what you're going to be doing.
3. Smile and nod, then take a slow, deep breath.
4. Hypnotize yourself and step inside your hypnotic reality.
5. If you've created a place for meditation, find your way there, and allow its name to resonate in your mind briefly. *K'ten*.
6. Find a nice spot to meditate, and do so.
7. When you've meditated enough, smile and say thank you to your place of meditation.
8. Wander out and back down the pathway to where you entered your hypnotic reality. Then continue on to bring yourself out of hypnosis.

If you keep a journal and you've made any discoveries that you'd like to record, it's a good idea to do that as soon as you've emerged from hypnosis.

Example 5 – Sleep

You've probably noticed by now that most the self-hypnosis instructions in this book end with *bring yourself out of hypnosis or drift off to sleep*.

Which one you choose depends on when you're doing it and what else you have on that day.

It's also possible to train yourself to fall asleep on demand using self-hypnosis.

Follow this process to do that:

1. Decide what time you're going to wake up, and check the current time so you know how long you're going to sleep.
2. Hypnotize yourself and step inside your hypnotic reality.
3. Explore your hypnotic reality in depth. Look at all the details. Be curious and fascinated. And calm and peaceful. Allow things to happen.
4. Look around for somewhere comfortable to lie down inside your hypnotic reality, then lie down there and make yourself comfortable.
5. Count down from 100 until you lose the numbers and drift off to sleep. Or just keep on exploring. It's your reality, so you can do whatever you choose.
6. Wake up at exactly the right time feeling refreshed, awake and alert.

As with meditation, if you keep a journal of your dreams or your sleep, write in it when you wake up.

Example 6 – Practicing self-hypnosis

So you've worked through the process. You can get into your own hypnotic reality. You've even set up time distortion so that you can have a lot more time there.

Why not supercharge it by practicing going into self-hypnosis when you're already inside your hypnotic reality?

If that sounds like the sort of thing you'd like to have happen, follow this process:

1. Hypnotize yourself and step inside your hypnotic reality.
2. Look around for somewhere comfortable to lie down inside your hypnotic reality, then lie down there and make yourself comfortable.
3. Hypnotize yourself inside your hypnotic reality, and enter into a second hypnotic reality.
4. Do stuff there.
5. Bring yourself out of the second hypnotic reality.
6. Repeat steps 3 to 5 as many times as you like to make it totally fluid.
7. Bring yourself out of the first hypnotic reality.

Once you can enter your hypnotic reality, it's possible to use this method to go from beginner to expert in the blink of an eye.

Example 7 – Hypnotic vacation

Now that you've got things working fluidly, you can really step it up. How about taking a full vacation inside your mind?

To do this, as with your place of meditation, write out a few sentences describing where your vacation will be and what you plan to do. Also write out how long you'll be there.

Choose a relatively small amount of time to spend on your vacation when you're starting out.

For example, if you're planning to be in hypnosis for an hour, start off by deciding to take a two hour vacation.

Make sure that you have an idea of what the places and events inside your vacation are like.

Then follow this process:

1. Read the plan you wrote out describing your hypnotic vacation and briefly imagine it to make it clear in your mind.
2. Hypnotize yourself and step inside your hypnotic reality.
3. Look around for a pathway.
4. Follow the pathway to the site of your dream vacation.
5. Do stuff there.
6. Wander back down the pathway to your hypnotic reality.
7. Bring yourself out of hypnosis.

Each time you go through this process, increase the amount of time that you plan to spend on vacation, while still spending the same amount of time out in the waking world.

By this I mean that if you are in hypnosis for an hour, on your first attempt you might aim to spend two hours on vacation. Once you've got that working, step it up to four hours the next time. Each time you achieve success, increase the duration of your vacation for the next time, until you reach the amount that you'd like.

Getting there is just a matter of consistent, deliberate practice.

Making it permanent

The key to making a permanent change inside the mind is just the same as the key to making memories stick: We have to be reminded to do it.

The way we do this is by finding something that we'll experience a lot, and then attaching the memory to it. This uses exactly the same underlying process as hypnotic symbols and anchors.

Essentially, when we think about two things at the same time, they become attached inside our minds. Then when we think of one of those things in the future, the other is reinforced. That's how our problems were installed in the first place, so we might as well use it to deinstall them!

So how do we do that?

If you look back over the processes in the examples, you'll see that we've already done it.

When we imagined ourselves talking to the cashier and feeling our shoulders relaxing, we implicitly attached the solution to the future as well.

The same thing happened when we saw ourselves playing the piano.

If you find that you can fix stuff with self-hypnosis, but the changes don't stick, it means that you need to do more of that part. When you're in hypnosis, add more positive details to make it more real. Run through the entire scenario more times to help your brain to learn. Allow yourself to feel positive emotions to help it to learn even more.

How to know it worked

So you've been through the entire process.

You've learnt how to hypnotize yourself.

You've learnt how to cause a change, whether it's fixing a problem, learning a skill, or something else entirely.

So how do you know it's worked?

First, with the hypnosis itself, the way you know it worked is that you worked through the steps. Sometimes you'll go deeper into hypnosis than other times. Each time you do it, you'll get better at it.

And before long, you'll be able to tell you're in hypnosis because it has its own distinct feel to it.

You will get faster each time.

After moving myself into hypnosis many, many thousands of times, all I have to do now is make a mental switch and I'm there in a second. With enough practice, you'll find the same thing. It's a skill that you learn like any other.

As for the changes, the way you tell that they've worked is by testing them. Make the change, then put yourself into the situation in real life and notice what's different. If you've done some work on social anxiety like in our example, go to the supermarket, talk to the cashier, and notice that your shoulders relax.

And for learning new skills, hopefully this one is obvious. Try doing the thing, and notice how much better you've become.

Conclusion

Congratulations!

If you've completed all the exercises in this book, you're now a self-hypnotist. As with every other skill you've ever learnt, the more you do it, the better you'll get at it.

I'd like to thank you for taking the time to make it to the end of this book. It's my hope that it has helped you.

If you've enjoyed this book, or learnt something from it, I'd really appreciate it if you could post a positive review.

This helps me out no end.

And if you're stuck on something, please feel free to reach out to me using the details on my website maxtrance.com.

It also helps me to update the book when I can see what parts don't make sense to people, which makes it better for future readers.

Next Steps

Did you know that it's possible to wake up inside your dreams and take control of them? This process is known as lucid dreaming, and it's been around for all of human history.

But there's a problem that lucid dreamers typically face. How exactly do you reliably wake up inside your dreams?

Now that you've learnt how to hypnotize yourself and step inside your own hypnotic reality, you're in an ideal position to extend your skill at self-hypnosis into supercharging your lucid dreams.

So how do you do it?

Remember the hypnotic reality that you stepped inside in the self-hypnosis process earlier in this book? I have no way of knowing how real that was inside your mind. Some people manage to experience full hypnotic realities that seem as real as real life, while others just have a dim sense of how things are.

If your hypnotic reality is a little less than perfect, getting there is a matter of practice, but it does take time and effort.

Lucid dreams are much the same thing as hypnotic realities. Only they seem completely real. And because they happen in your sleep, you can claim back at least some of the 20 or more years that we lose to sleep in a typical human lifetime.

To supercharge your lucid dreams, all you have to do is look around inside your hypnotic reality for a pathway into your lucid dream, follow that pathway, and step inside, allowing the dream to form around you.

When you do this, you get two huge benefits. First, the time distortion from the self-hypnosis is still in effect. This has been known to cause us to perceive large amounts of time inside our dreams. And second, with a little practice you can step directly into your lucid dream from being awake.

If you'd like to learn more about lucid dreaming, I cover it in detail in my book **Lucid: How to Start Lucid Dreaming Even If You Never Remember Your Dreams**.

Follow Max Trance Online

Facebook Page: **https://fb.me/theMaxTrance**

Facebook Messenger: **https://m.me/theMaxTrance**

Instagram: **https://ig.me/theMaxTrance**

Website: **https://maxtrance.com**

Also by Max Trance

Artful Hypnotic Anchoring
A guide on how to construct and use hypnotic anchors. Available as an eBook and in paperback.

Hypnosis Quick Start Guide
Step by step instructions designed to take you from complete beginner to hypnotizing your first subject. Available as an eBook and in paperback.

Hypnosis Quick Start Workbook
Mostly the same as the Hypnosis Quick Start Guide, only with spaces to write out your answers to the questions I've found to be important to ask when you would like to become good at hypnosis. Available in paperback.

Lucid: How to Start Lucid Dreaming Even if You Never Remember Your Dreams
Step by step instructions designed to take you from complete beginner to experiencing your first lucid dream and remembering it in vivid detail, even if you've never been able to recall your dreams before. Available as an eBook and in paperback.

Lucid Dreaming Planner and Journal
The Dream Planner and Journal specifically designed to be used with the material in my introduction to lucid dreaming: Lucid. Available in paperback.

10 More Fun Things to Do With Hypnosis
Additional hypnotic phenomena to use with the processes in the Hypnosis Quick Start books. Available as an eBook from maxtrance.com/10more.

The Lucid Dreaming Formula: How to Wake Up Inside Your Dreams and Remember Them

Designed to be the quickest possible introduction to lucid dreaming, this short book covers the two essential skills that you must have if you would like to experience lucid dreams. Available as an eBook from maxtrance.com/ldf.

The Quit Smoking Formula

This one is designed to be a complete quit smoking program in book form. Inside you'll find the processes that I use to help smokers quit for life. Only re-organized so that they can be implemented with self-hypnosis. Available as an eBook from maxtrance.com/qsf.

The Two Page Deep Trance Script

Want a script that I've used to quickly guide the most resistant subjects into deep hypnosis? This short script was specifically designed to do just that. Available as an eBook.

Don't Forget the Zombies: The Zombie Apocalypse Hypnosis Script

Want to help your friends to believe they lived through a zombie apocalypse then have them tell you all about it? This book was specifically designed to show you how to do just that. Available as an eBook and in paperback.

Made in the USA
Thornton, CO
12/27/23 00:16:56

d362260a-bfd7-44f0-8976-c9b2b2737616R03